WALKING

IN THE

LIGHT OF FAITH

Walking in the Light of Faith

James H. Kroeger

Walking in the Light of Faith
Copyright © 2014 by James H. Kroeger

Artwork: Anthony Capirayan

Library of Congress Cataloging-in-Publication Data

Kroeger, James H.
> Walking in the Light of Faith
>> p. x + 74   cm. 21 x 13.7
>> ISBN: 978-971-004-194-7

> 1.   Catholic Church—Doctrines. 2. Theology, Doctrinal—Popular Works. 3. Catholic Church—Year of Faith.
> I. Title. II. Kroeger, James H.

>> BX 1754 K76 2014
>> 230.2—dc21

Published in 2014 by

ST PAULS
7708 St. Paul Road, San Antonio Village
1203 Makati City, Philippines
Tel. (632) 88959701 to 04 • (632) 88966771
Fax. (632) 88907131
Website: www.stpauls.ph
E-mail for orders: wholesale@stpauls.ph

Printing Information:
Current Printing: first digit

2	3	4	5	6

Year of current printing: first year shown

2019	2020	2021	2022	2023

ST PAULS is an apostolate of the priests and brothers of the SOCIETY OF ST. PAUL who proclaim the Gospel through the media of social communication.

CONTENTS

HOLY SPIRIT

Introduction

Every year must be a Year of Faith reflects the vision of Pope Benedict XVI in summoning the Church to a *special* "Year of Faith" during 2011-2012. At his Sunday Mass on October 16, 2011, the Pope noted that this special year (and every year) should be "a moment of grace and commitment to a more complete conversion to God, to strengthen our faith in Him, and proclaim Him with joy to the people of our time."

Pope Benedict's formal apostolic letter on the Year of Faith, *Porta Fidei* (The Door of Faith) was dated October 11, 2011, the anniversary of the opening of the Second Vatican Council on October 11, 1962. Quoting the words of Saint John Paul II, Benedict asserts that even in our time the documents of Vatican II *"have lost nothing of their value or brilliance…*. I feel more than ever in duty bound to point to the Council as *the great grace bestowed on the Church in the twentieth century*: there we find a sure compass by which to take our bearings" (PF 5).

In *Porta Fidei* Benedict lists three specific reasons for instituting the Year of Faith: that Christians *profess the faith* with fuller conviction, *deepen their encounter with Jesus Christ* especially in the Eucharist, and *witness the faith* more credibly in their daily life.

When the Year of Faith concluded, Pope Francis gifted the Church with his first encyclical, *Lumen Fidei* (The Light of Faith). Again, Francis linked the faith of contemporary Catholics with Vatican II. "The Year of Faith was inaugurated on the fiftieth anniversary of the opening of the Second Vatican Council. This is itself a clear indication that Vatican II was a Council on faith" (LF 6).

Pope Francis advises us: "Faith consists in the willingness to let ourselves be constantly transformed and renewed by God's call" (LF 13). "Faith does not merely gaze at Jesus, but sees things as Jesus himself sees them, with his own eyes: it is a participation in his way of seeing" (LF 18).

Friends, this small booklet you hold in your hands is a compilation of the sixty "vignettes of faith" that appeared in the weekly missalette *Sambuhay*, extending over the fourteen months of the Year of Faith. Readers, use this book for your personal growth, spiritual meditation, and deeper insight into your own "journey of faith." You are invited to "pray" these short reflections, echoing the urgent plea of a desperate father to Jesus for his dying son: "Lord, I believe. Help my unbelief" (Mk 9:24).

Finally, Pope Francis encourages us to turn in prayer to Mary, our Mother in Faith: "Mother, help our faith! ... Sow in our faith the joy of the Risen One. Remind us that those who believe are never alone. Teach us to see all things with the eyes of Jesus, that he may be light for our path" (LF 60).

James H. Kroeger, MM
Pentecost 2014

Introducing the "Year of Faith"

Pope Benedict XVI announced on October 16, 2011 that the entire Church would celebrate a "Year of Faith." It extended from October 11, 2012 (fiftieth anniversary of the opening of the Second Vatican Council) until November 24, 2013 (Solemnity of Christ the King).

The pope outlined the purpose of this special year; it is "to give fresh impetus to the mission of the whole Church to lead human beings out of the wilderness in which they often find themselves to the place of life, friendship with Christ that gives us life in fullness."

Benedict XVI added that the year would be "a moment of grace and commitment to a more complete conversion to God, to strengthen our faith in Him and proclaim Him with joy to the people of our time."

The pope envisioned this conversion as opening the "door of faith" (Acts 14:27). As Catholics, the door of faith was opened at our baptism; we are called to open it again, walk through it, and rediscover and renew our relationship with Christ and the Church.

Retrieving the Treasures of Vatican II

The opening day of the "Year of Faith" declared by Pope Benedict XVI coincided with the fiftieth anniversary of the opening of the Second Vatican Council (October 11, 1962-2012), the greatest religious event of the past century.

During the "Year of Faith" Catholics were asked to study and reflect upon the sixteen documents of Vatican II as well as to explore the *Catechism of the Catholic Church*. This effort focuses on a deepened knowledge and commitment to live one's faith.

In *Porta Fidei* 5 (Door of Faith), Benedict XVI's apostolic letter, the pope, quoting John Paul II, asserts that the texts of Vatican II "have lost nothing of their value or brilliance.... I feel more than ever duty bound to point to the Council as *the great grace bestowed on the Church in the twentieth century*: there we find a sure compass by which to take our bearings in the century now beginning." Vatican II "can become increasingly powerful for the ever necessary renewal of the Church."

POPE BENEDICT XVI

• 3 •

Mission Demands Deep Faith

In his message for World Mission Sunday 2013, Pope Benedict XVI noted that the celebration this year "has a very special meaning" since it was at Vatican II (50 years ago) that the Church defined herself by asserting that "the pilgrim Church is missionary by her very nature" (AG 2). Benedict XVI noted that mission "must be the constant horizon and paradigm of every ecclesial endeavor." This task demands profound faith.

Already Pope John Paul II had stated: "*Mission is an issue of faith,* an accurate indicator of our faith in Christ and his love for us" (RM 11). He goes on to say that "in the Church's history, missionary drive has always been a sign of vitality, just as its lessening is a sign of a crisis of faith" (RM 2). "The Lord is always calling us to come out of ourselves and to share with others the goods we possess, starting with the most precious gift of all—our faith" (RM 49).

Saint Pedro Calungsod, faith-filled Filipino missionary-martyr (canonized on Mission Sunday 2013), intercede that the Philippine Church will always be a dynamic missionary Church.

• 4 •

Pope Benedict Speaks on Faith

The thought of Benedict XVI on the topic of faith is extremely rich. A few short quotes manifest some of the pope's key insights.

In *Deus Caritas Est* (39), he writes: "Faith tells us that God has given his Son for our sakes and gives us the victorious certainty that it is really true: God is love! It thus transforms our impatience and our doubts into the sure hope that God holds the world in his hands...."

For Benedict in *Spe Salvi* (7) "Faith is not merely a personal reaching out towards things to come that are still totally absent: it gives us something.... Faith draws the future into the present...." We already share in the promised gifts and new life of God!

In a homily for the close of the Year for Priests (June 11, 2010) the pope called Mary the "great woman of faith and love who has become in every generation a wellspring of faith, love and life." Benedict echoes the words of Elizabeth to Mary: "Yes, blessed is she who believed that the promise made her by the Lord would be fulfilled" (Lk 1:45).

• 5 •

Faith: God's Gracious Gift

Succinctly stated, faith is a free gift from God, a grace, an undeserved beneficence bestowed gratuitously by a loving God. Saint Paul was profoundly aware that he did not deserve to have faith and be an apostle, "but by God's grace that is what I am, and the grace that he gave me has not been fruitless" (1 Cor 15:9-10).

We admit that one does not deserve or earn the gift of faith; yet, we respond to God's loving initiative by a free and personal act. Our response can be captured in three words, all beginning with the letter "r." Faith is all about profoundly *recognizing* God's inestimable gift in sending his Son for our salvation.

With grateful hearts, a Christian focuses on *receiving* the gift of faith and personally integrating it into one's life. The recognition and reception of the gift—particularly the person of Christ—overflow in concrete efforts to share this faith and love with others, *reciprocating* God's love in Jesus through deeds of compassion and missionary service. Faith, a special gift, is our precious possession!

• 6 •

Exploring the Meaning of Faith

During the "Year of Faith" proclaimed by Pope Benedict XVI, Catholics were asked to delve deeply into the meaning and dimensions of the gift of faith. A simple description offered by A. Dulles is: "Faith is the basic act or disposition by which human beings respond to revelation and enter into a saving relationship with God."

In traditional theology, faith was clarified with two helpful terms: *fides quae* and *fides qua*. *Fides quae* ("faith which") refers to the knowledge and acceptance of revealed truth as content, teaching, doctrine, or dogma. Catholics are familiar with both the Apostles' and Nicene Creeds used in the liturgy; they describe the content of the essential truths of the faith.

Fides qua ("faith by which") refers to a personal, self-surrendering act of trust to a personal God who reveals his inner divine life and invites individuals into a personal relationship of communion and friendship. In short, as described by the *Youcat* 21 [*Youth Catechism*]: "*Faith* is both *knowledge* and *trust*."

Contemporary Reflection on Faith

The richness of faith is explored in theology today. The valid insights into faith [incorporating both *dogmatic teaching* as well as *personal surrender* to a loving God] are certainly retained. The intellectualist [knowing Church teaching] and the fiducial [personal relationship with God] always remain essential for believers.

While contemporary theological reflection certainly incorporates these two dimensions, it also places emphasis on a third aspect of faith. One might term this third dimension the "missionary" or "witnessing" dimension of faith. One's faith-encounter with God leads to active witness and evangelization.

In short, faith demands: (1) entrusting oneself to God, (2) knowledge and acceptance of Church teaching, *and* (3) a vigorous commitment to spread the faith, to "tell the world of his love"! Indeed, where one or another of these three characteristics is lacking, faith must be judged to be immature or imperfect. Christian faith is always a missionary faith!

Faith: Three Essential Elements

In fidelity to the call of Benedict XVI during this "Year of Faith," several reflections on the rich meaning of faith have already been offered in this catechesis series. Indeed, a wide variety of terms and images can provide insight into God's gift of faith. Is a simple synthesis or schema possible? Faith always includes:

A: INTELLECTUAL and NOTIONAL — *informative* — HEAD — *Doctrine*

B: AFFECTIVE and FIDUCIAL — *formative/ transformative* — HEART — *Devotion*

C: CONCRETIZED in DEEDS-WITNESS — *performative* — HANDS — *Deeds*

In his encyclical *Spe Salvi* [2, 4, 10] Pope Benedict XVI frequently asserts that the Christian message and faith must be "not only 'informative' but 'performative'." The pope asks: Does our faith "make things happen"? Is it really "life-changing"? We all ask ourselves: How mature and complete is my faith? We pray with the apostles: "Lord, increase our faith" (Lk 17:5).

MARY MEETS ELIZABETH

• 9 •

"Nothing is Impossible for God"

People of faith who surrender to God's will radically accept that "nothing is impossible for God." This attitude is seen in the lives of two "Biblical Saints," Zechariah and Elizabeth. Though they were "blameless" in God's sight, "they were childless; Elizabeth was barren and they were both advanced in years" (Lk 1:5-7).

Zechariah, a priest serving at the Jerusalem temple, experiences a vision. An angel tells him that his wife will conceive a son; he doubts the prophecy. Yet, after returning home, Elizabeth conceived (Lk 1:24); she says: "The Lord has done this for me" (Lk 1:25).

Mary visits the elderly couple; when she spoke the babe in Elizabeth's womb "leapt for joy" (Lk 1:41). When the babe is born and is named John, Zechariah praises God in his *Benedictus* (Lk 1:68-79), proclaiming the "tender mercies of our God" (Lk 1:78).

Zechariah and Elizabeth remained "faith-full" even in their childlessness; God rewarded them. In "impossible" situations, do we still affirm that "nothing is impossible for God"?

• 10 •

John the Baptist and Faith

Each year during the Advent season, the Church asks us to reflect on the life of John the Baptist, his preaching, his imprisonment, even his martyrdom. The Baptist's story can deepen our faith, enriching our preparation for Christmas.

John preaches: "Repent, for the kingdom of heaven is close at hand…. If you are repentant, produce the appropriate fruit" (Mt 3:2, 8). "Prepare the way of the Lord; make straight his paths" (Mk 1:3).

John points us to Jesus: "Look, there is the lamb of God who takes away the sins of the world" (Jn 1:29). "He must increase, I must decrease" (Jn 3:30).

The figure of John the Baptist is significant because he directs our attention, not to himself, but to Jesus. In the same way, our ongoing renewal will bear fruit, not because we, through our own efforts alone, have initiated a program of penance and renewal, but because we have more deeply surrendered in faith to Jesus himself, the real source of all grace and renewal, the true center of all faith.

• 11 •

Our Mother of Faith

Saint Luke, "Mary's biographer," notes twice in his Gospel that Mary "treasured all these things and pondered them in her heart" (Lk 2:19, 51). This attitude of deep faith can be captured in three simple Latin words from Scripture: FIAT, STABAT, MAGNIFICAT.

FIAT (Lk 1:38) is Mary's "yes" response to Angel Gabriel's invitation to become the Mother of God. *Fiat voluntas tua*; let it be done to me according to your will. This was Mary's unconditional, definitive self-surrender; she made "countless *fiat*s" throughout her life.

STABAT (Jn 19:25) describes Mary's "standing" faithfully under the cross. Perhaps, this was Mary's "supreme *fiat.*" She was faithful to the end.

MAGNIFICAT (Lk 1:46) expresses Mary's praising or magnifying the Lord—not only in the joyful moments of life, but at all times and in all events.

Mary's example of faith inspires us to give an enduring **yes** to **stand** faithfully, **praising** God in all life's challenges.

• 12 •

Joseph: Pillar of Enduring Faith

In guiding the Holy Family, Joseph acts with complete confidence and total surrender to God's will. His life, like ours, involved fatiguing labors, ambiguous situations, and difficult decisions.

Joseph's faith and trust were severely tested when he realized that Mary was pregnant and they had not had relations. His anguish is relieved when he learns from the angel that "what is conceived in her is of the Holy Spirit" (Mt 1:20). In genuine faith, Joseph immediately receives Mary into his home.

The birth of Jesus under very primitive circumstances in Bethlehem must have caused Joseph great pain and tested his faith. Yet, Joseph accompanies Mary in a total acceptance of the divine will.

As the Holy Family hurriedly escapes like refugees into Egypt without any preparations, Joseph's faith is challenged. Then, when King Herod dies, the family has to once again relocate to Nazareth. Indeed, Joseph's faith was often tested; yet, he trusted God. He is a model of faith for all—in all things.

• 13 •

Faith: A Universal Gift

Each January the Church celebrates the Epiphany, which means "manifestation" or "appearance." The Magi or "wise men" visit and pay homage to Jesus. This feast, sometimes called the "Gentile Christmas," is Christ's manifestation to Gentiles (non-Jews).

In his Gospel Matthew is not merely recording historical data about the Magi; he is communicating a theological truth. In short, Epiphany celebrates that the gift of faith is for *all* people of *all* nations. The treasure of faith in Christ belongs equally to all who freely accept it, Jew and Gentile, slave or free, male or female (cf. Gal 3:26-29).

Luke's Gospel narrates the appearance of Christ to the lowly, poor, unlearned shepherds. Matthew's Gospel reveals Christ to wise men who bring very costly gifts. Indeed, faith is for *all* persons, for *everyone*, without distinction!

We *must* share our faith with others. Pope Paul VI said it well: "Others may be able to be saved without hearing the gospel, but can we be saved if we neglect to preach it?"

• 14 •

Baptism: Origin of Faith and Mission

The Baptism of Jesus is accorded much importance in the Gospels; it is recorded by all three synoptic evangelists. Questions may arise about the need for Jesus to be baptized. However, the "necessity" question is *not* the focus of the Gospel writers.

The fundamental interpretation of the event is that it is the formal approval and commissioning by the Father of his beloved Son Jesus for his public ministry. Jesus experiences his call to mission; he is grasped and affirmed by the Spirit of God coming upon him. He is recognized as God's chosen servant and Son. The public ministry of Jesus begins; he calls people to faith.

In our baptism *all Christians* have received the marvelous gift of faith through the Holy Spirit. Genuine faith is active and dynamic, always manifested in "mission" responses. If our faith-commitment is a bit half-hearted, let us renew our baptismal mission to spread faith in Jesus. We join Jesus in his faith-filled mission commitment.

• 15 •

Santo Niño and Adult Faith

At Christmastime Christians celebrate the infant Christ-child lying in the manger. This image confirms that Jesus became human and was born of the Virgin Mary. We are drawn irresistibly to the child and his mother. The tender scene evokes and strengthens our faith. We recognize the *absolute truth*: out of self-sacrificing love, God has become one with all humanity.

Evangelists Matthew and Luke narrate the events surrounding Jesus' birth. However, is that all there is? Is the story only about the infant Christ? Is faith focused on a sentimental attraction to the baby Jesus?

Biblical exegetes like Raymond Brown assert that we must include the "adult Christ"—even at Christmastime! Yes, the yearly feast of Sto. Niño *consoles* us, but it also *confronts*, *challenges*, and *converts* us. We need to live with adult faith in a world of poverty, injustice, and suffering, a world hungry for love. Can the love and faith we feel for the Sto. Niño empower us to engage the world— as adults with the tender love of the divine child?

• 16 •

Faith for Ordinary Times

The longest "season" in the Church's liturgical calendar is "ordinary time." "Ordinary" implies the uneventful, the "nothing special" season of the year. After weeks of intense "Christmas" celebrations, we settle into regular, daily life—yes, into the ordinary.

There is a profound connection between major feasts and ordinary, daily life. Because of Christ's coming, no time is ordinary; all time takes on new significance. Ordinary daily existence has been profoundly transformed; it has become *Christic*, renewed by Christ's birth.

As faith-filled people we realize that our lives—even life itself—are filled with routine, repetitive, monotonous, ordinary activities. Herein lies our vocation and mission. We are called to be "saints of the ordinary"—*walking in faith* through life's ordinary events.

Blessed Mother Teresa of Calcutta has said: "We cannot do great things; we can only do ordinary things with great love." We need deep faith to transform life's ordinary events into moments of grace, faith-filled encounters with God.

• 17 •

Creeds: Concise Expressions of Faith

Catholics are very familiar with "creeds." They were pronounced at one's baptism; they were memorized in preparation for first Holy Communion; they are used in the liturgy on all Sundays and major feast days of the Church.

The English word "creed" derives from the Latin *credo*, "I believe." Creeds have been highly developed within Christianity; yet, they also exist in other faith traditions. For example, Islam has the *Shahada*, which asserts that God alone is God and that Muhammad is God's messenger.

As an expression of faith, one finds simple confessions in the New Testament: "Jesus is Lord" (1 Cor 12:3), "Jesus Christ our Lord" (Rom 1:4), "Father, Son and Holy Spirit" (Mt 28:19). The early Church gradually fashioned much fuller expressions of the faith.

The two creeds most familiar to Christians are the Apostles' Creed and the Nicene Creed. For Eucharistic celebrations both of these traditional creeds are approved for use.

• 18 •

The Apostles' Creed

The Apostles' Creed is clearly the fruit of Christian tradition and faith, developed over the centuries. Its exact origins cannot be pinpointed; it may have its roots in an Old Roman Creed. Charlemagne (742-814) adopted it and imposed it upon his empire, leading to Rome's approval of this creedal formula.

Clearly, the structure of the Apostles' Creed is determined by the Trinitarian nature of Christian faith. The "Great Commission" of Matthew's Gospel (28:18-20) speaks of baptism "in the name of the Father and of the Son and of the Holy Spirit." The concluding verse of Paul's second letter to the Corinthians (13:13) contains this salutation (so familiar as the greeting found in the introductory rites of the Mass): "The grace of our Lord Jesus Christ, the love of God, and the communion of the Holy Spirit be with you all."

The shortest "creed" in Church use is the "Sign of the Cross." It affirms Trinitarian faith and is used to sanctify daily life; it is common in the liturgy and in the blessing of persons and objects.

• 19 •

The Nicene Creed

The profession of faith, popularly known as the Nicene Creed (name derived from the Council of Nicaea in 325), is actually the creed affirmed by the Council of Constantinople in 381. Technically, it should be called the "Nicene-Constantinopolitan Creed."

Based on the creed issued at Nicaea, this Trinitarian formula of faith is considerably longer; it includes a fuller treatment of the Holy Spirit, affirming the full divine status of the Holy Spirit.

The Latin text of this creed used by the Church in the West adds the phrase, "and the Son" (Latin, *Filioque*). Thus, the creed affirms that the Holy Spirit "proceeds from the Father and the Son."

Historical details and linguistic nuances have helped clarify the faith. However, the recitation of the creed should focus us on *our personal relationship with God*. Genuine faith engages not only the intellect, but also our heart, indeed our entire person. We profess belief in a *personal God*, in the three Persons in God: Father, Son, and Holy Spirit.

• 20 •

Creeds and Deeds: Expressions of Faith

The Christian faith is expressed in various creedal formulas; it must also be convincingly expressed in Christ-like deeds of service. A true story from an African missionary shows how generous service communicates faith.

A young teacher who was a Catholic was dying of AIDS. His own sister was the only person who cared for him; other family and village members kept their distance, due to fear. The teacher advised his sister (not a Christian) to approach the Christian community and to pray with them.

She joined the Christians in their Mass on Sunday; she told them about her brother's situation. That same week some Catholics came to visit the man. They brought food and prayed with him. They came every week and were with him as he died.

The young woman continued: "When my brother died, not one of our family or village came to bury my brother. They were all afraid. The Christians washed his body and buried him." With deep emotion, the woman said: "I want to be one of them, Padre! I am now a believer!"

SERVING WITH COMPASSION

• 21 •

"Abba" Reveals Jesus' Identity

Christian creeds address God as "the Father, the almighty." Calling God "Father" is a personal address, asserting his care for all creation, especially for all humanity.

God's fatherly care for his people is already found in the Old Testament (cf. Deut 7:6-9); however, Jesus reveals a totally new and profound meaning to addressing God as "Father." God is called Father 170 times in the Gospels [Mark (4); Luke (15); Matthew (42); John (109)].

God's fatherhood is a clear hallmark of Jesus' life and prayer. Frequently, Jesus prays to his *Abba*. He calls God "my Father" (Mt 11:26; Lk 10:21). His mission is from the Father (cf. Jn 11:41-42). During the last supper he addresses his Father (cf. Jn 17:1, 5, 11, 21, 24, 25). Jesus turned to his *Abba* in the crisis moments of his life: Gethsemane (cf. Mk 14:36; Mt 26:42), Calvary (cf. Lk 23:34). His dying words are: "Father, into your hands I commend by spirit" (Lk 23:46).

In short, Jesus' *abba*-consciousness reveals his identity as God's true Son—a core dogma of Christian faith.

• 22 •

God: Our Compassionate Father

Known worldwide, Jesus' parable about a father and his two sons (cf. Lk 15:11-32) expresses dramatically God's tender compassion for his children—for us! The "prodigal son" story is often called the parable of the "compassionate father." Marvelously, the narrative expresses a core element of Christian faith: divine mercy reflects God's true nature.

The prodigal son squanders more than material goods; he compromises his very dignity as a son in his father's house. Yet, God as Father remains steadfast in his love and affection for his wayward, yet repentant, son.

This parable shows that God's mercy can reach down to every prodigal son, to each human person. God's manner of acting does not humiliate the erring person; his mercy restores the individual to his true value—as a beloved child of God.

Divine mercy is manifested in this heart-warming parable. Christian faith asserts God's forgiving compassion—better expressed in this story than ever could be captured in a dogmatic statement!

• 23 •

Rich in Mercy

Saint Pope John Paul II wrote fourteen encyclicals; three of them focus on one person of the Trinity: Father, Son and Spirit. *Dives in Misericordia* (Rich in Mercy) is focused on "the Father of compassion and God of all consolation" (2 Cor 1:3). Undoubtedly, our God is "rich in mercy" (Eph 2:4).

This 1980 encyclical is a "heartfelt appeal by the Church to mercy, which humanity and the modern world need so much" (2). The pope asserts that "the Church must consider it one of her principal duties—at every stage of history and especially in our modern age—to proclaim and to introduce into life the mystery of mercy" (14).

The more today's world loses the sense of God's profound mercy, "the more the Church has the right and duty to appeal to the God of mercy" (15). Living one's faith demands a close imitation of the Father's mercy.

A concluding reflective question: What epitaph might be written on your tombstone? How beautiful if the inscription read that during your lifetime you were always "rich in mercy"!

• 24 •

Faith: Shaped by the Paschal Mystery

All human life has a paschal configuration; simply, this means that our life patterns continually move *through death to renewed life.* Human existence clearly reflects a "paschal paradigm." We struggle to move through darkness to light, through captivity to freedom, through suffering and brokenness to wholeness, from loneliness to communion, from sin to grace and new life.

Faith-filled Christians struggle to follow the path traced out for us by Christ in his paschal mystery. Each year during Holy Week we walk—in deep faith—with our suffering savior. We enter with Christ into his passion and death; through his resurrection we share joyously in his new life.

Living the paschal mystery in daily life demands profound faith, an intimate relationship with our suffering-risen savior. We encounter Christ in his redemptive paschal mystery; we also strive to be in solidarity with all humanity on its path of suffering. Indeed, living as a "paschal Christian" requires much more than a superficial faith!

• 25 •

Exsultet! Rejoice! Jesus Lives!

At the core of Christian faith is the Resurrection. Saint Paul clearly states: "If Christ has not been raised then our preaching is useless and your believing is also useless" (1 Cor 15:14). Indeed, our Christian faith stands or falls on the Resurrection.

To appreciate the beauty of resurrection faith, one could reflect on the "divine reversal" that happens at Easter. What appeared as death's victory on Good Friday is reversed by Christ's triumph over the grave. In his paschal mystery Christ takes humanity's pride and sinfulness and changes them into an opportunity for grace; God does not return evil for offense committed against him; he answers with love. Adam's sin that brought death is reversed by Christ's humble obedience—even unto death—to achieve life and salvation for all.

God shows he is God by giving us his own Son as our crucified-risen Savior. Marvel at the unfathomable love of God! Marvel at this resurrection mystery—and believe!

CHRIST, RISEN IN GLORY

• 26 •

Does Doubt Mix with Faith?

The apostle Thomas is probably the most well-known "doubter." He demands that he touch Christ's wounds—before he accept that Jesus is risen (cf. Jn 20:19-29). Are faith and doubt related?

Before becoming pope, Benedict XVI noted in his *Introduction to Christianity* that "the believer is always threatened with an uncertainty that in moments of temptation can suddenly and unexpectedly cast a piercing light on the fragility of the whole [faith] that usually seems so self-evident to him."

Indeed, believers do not live immune to doubts in a kind of self-sufficient life. The book *Mother Teresa: Come Be My Light* by Brian Kolodiejchuk shows how this "living saint" struggled with darkness and doubts. She drew some consolation from the awareness that her suffering was a partaking in what Christ endured on the cross. Even in her darkness, Mother Teresa kept faith with the poor and suffering whom she served.

Blessed Mother Teresa of Calcutta, help us to believe—even in moments of darkness.

• 27 •

Telling God's Love Story in Faith

Saint James boldly states: "Faith is like that: if good works do not go with it, it is quite dead" (Jas 2:17). What we affirm as Christians in our **creeds** we must manifest in our **deeds**. Faith without mission and service is quite dead! Recall the lives of two Filipino missionaries who told the story of God's love—through lives of service and martyrdom.

Jesuit scholastic Richie Fernando gave his life in Cambodia in 1996, as he saved many handicapped students from a grenade attack. Shortly before his death he e-mailed a close friend: "I know where my heart is ... it is with Jesus Christ.... I want to be like Christ. I will follow Jesus."

Claretian Missionary Rhoel Gallardo was abducted in Basilan in 2000 by the Abu Sayyaf, held captive for 43 days, tortured and killed. Yet, he never surrendered his faith; he constantly encouraged his fellow Christian hostages. His death at age 34 was a shining witness of God's love.

These missionaries were examples of deep faith and God's love in practice.

• 28 •

Lord, Be My Good Shepherd

During the Easter season the Church celebrates our risen Good Shepherd who willingly laid down his life for the sheep of his flock.

In this context, allow your imagination to recall the time of the early Christians in Rome when their faith was severely tested. Both Saints Peter and Paul were martyred between 64 and 67 under the persecution of Emperor Nero. Christians were being thrown to the lions in the coliseum. In a word, being a Christian demanded deep faith—even to the point of death.

The Christians often literally went "underground"; they met in the catacombs to worship and bury their dead. What paintings did these Christians place on the catacomb walls? The most frequent image was that of the Good Shepherd. Even in the most difficult of times, Christians felt Jesus' closeness. Quite naturally we say (along with the early Christians): "The Lord is my Shepherd." Jesus' presence guides us in the midst of all our fears and sufferings. Our faith is indeed a great source of consolation!

"AS I" – True Measure of Authentic Faith

There is only one criterion against which to judge how authentically we live our faith: the person of Jesus our Lord.

Two passages spoken by Jesus at the last supper direct us to the heart of the matter: "I give you a new commandment: love one another; just *AS I* have loved you, you must also love one another" (Jn 13:34, cf. 15:10, 15:12, 15:17). "If I, therefore, the master and teacher, have washed your feet, you ought to wash one another's feet. I have given you a model to follow, so that *AS I* have done for you, you should also do" (Jn 13:14-15).

Both passages form a unity. Jesus gives his commandment of love, then puts it into practice by washing his disciples' feet. He challenges them to do the same. Notice the parallel words: *AS I*. Indeed, Jesus asserts that he is the model, criterion, and measure of "faith-in-action."

Those very simple words "*AS I*" (three letters of the alphabet) must guide our daily decisions and actions. How eminently clear! How difficult and challenging!

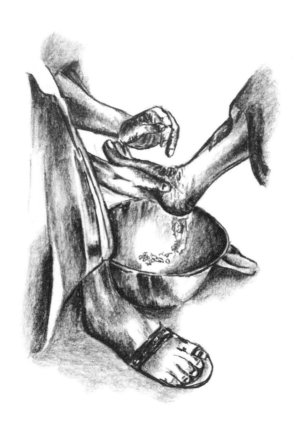

HUMBLE, GENUINE SERVICE

• 30 •

Fruits of the Year of Faith

The Church's Year of Faith declared by Pope Benedict was an opportune moment to take stock of our progress in faith.

Faith is all about being in relationship with Jesus Christ; thus, we honestly admit that before we can evangelize (share our faith with others) we must be first evangelized (deepen our own personal faith in Christ). Pope Paul VI noted: "The Church is an evangelizer, but she begins by being evangelized herself…. The Church is evangelized by constant conversion and renewal in order to evangelize the world with credibility" (EN 15).

With honesty we ask: Where is Christ in my life? Am I more fervent in my participation in the Eucharist? Do I take time to pray? Do I read the scriptures to better love Jesus and allow him to enlighten my decisions? What "faith-witness" do I give to my family members, friends, and coworkers?

Do not miss Benedict XVI's invitation to open the "door of faith," to walk through it, and rediscover and renew your relationship with Christ and his Church.

• 31 •

Paschal Mystery: Core of Christian Faith

The "paschal mystery" refers to the unified total events of Christ's passion, death, resurrection, ascension, and the sending of the Holy Spirit. The term encompasses God's entire, loving plan of salvation for all people. The roots of this expression are from the Greek word *pascha* and Hebrew *pesah*, meaning "passover" and from the Greek *musterion*, meaning "secret reality" or "rite."

Clearly the term reflects the Hebrew Passover, which was Yahweh's act of delivering Israel from Egyptian slavery, anticipating God's salvific action in the entire Christ event. In the "paschal mystery" Christ "passed over" to the Father, drawing all humanity with him.

In our baptism we were initiated into this saving mystery of Christ's dying and rising (cf. Rom 6:3-5). At each Eucharist we remember, celebrate and partake of Christ's Paschal Mystery (cf. 1 Cor 11:23-26). When we proclaim the "mystery of faith" at Mass after the consecration, we are affirming our profound faith in Christ's Paschal Mystery.

• 32 •

The Spirit and Seven Special Gifts

The Holy Spirit, above all else, is *the* gift (cf. Jn 14:26), the source of all comfort and grace; he proceeds from the Father and the Son. The Spirit is the sanctifier and giver of gifts; through the Spirit the Church receives ordinary, hierarchical, charismatic, and sacramental gifts; the Spirit invites us all to holiness and salvation.

Catholic tradition also speaks of seven spiritual favors or benefits bestowed by the Spirit, commonly known as the Gifts of the Holy Spirit. These are the gifts that Isaiah prophesied would dwell in their fullness in the Messiah: *wisdom, understanding, counsel, fortitude, knowledge, piety,* and *fear of the Lord* (cf. Is 11:1-3).

These gifts are fully manifested in Jesus at his baptism; subsequently, these gifts are bestowed on the disciples of Jesus at Pentecost. As we receive these gifts at baptism and throughout our lives, we believe in faith that they enable us to be docile to the promptings of God's Spirit. A Christian is a Spirit-filled disciple of Jesus.

• 33 •

Trinity: Faith in God's "Tri-Unity"

The Church's teaching on the Trinity defines God to be formed of three divine persons, Father, Son and Holy Spirit. All three persons are co-equal, co-substantial, and co-eternal. Indeed, within the unity of one God, there are three separate persons, all co-equal in power, nature and eternity.

In sacred scripture, Jesus boldly proclaims, "The Father and I are One" (Jn 10:30). Jesus also speaks of "the Advocate, the Holy Spirit, whom the Father will send in my name" (Jn 14:26). Jesus sends forth his disciples to baptize people "in the name of the Father and of the Son and of the Holy Spirit" (Mt 28:19).

Faith in the Trinity invites gratitude from us, since we are baptized into this Trinitarian faith; God enables us to share in the love and dynamism of his own inner life. The Trinity can also provide a model for the ideal human community, in which people, united by mutual love, work together in harmonious consensus, and the equality and dignity of each person is treasured and respected.

• 34 •

Eucharistic Faith: Christ's True Presence

Catholics believe that Jesus Christ is truly present in the Eucharist in his body and blood, humanity and divinity, under the form of bread and wine. This real presence flows from Christ's total self-gift on the cross; his presence effects communion with His Church through His body and blood.

Some years ago, while serving in a rural Mindanao parish, I had a powerful experience from an unexpected source that reminded me of Christ's Eucharistic presence. Catalino, a man of about thirty years who only had the mind of a child, liked to be around the parish rectory (*convento*); no one objected to his presence. He was friendly and liked to talk to everyone.

Catalino would often ask me for some bread, cookies, or crackers. He normally was present at Mass and would reverently go to communion. One day (to satisfy *my* doubts) I decided to ask: "Catalino, when you are in Church and go to get something to eat, what is that? Is it a special cookie or cracker?" Immediately he responded: "Oh no, Father. ***That's Jesus!***"

• 35 •

Pope Benedict's Profession of Faith

During his final General Audience Benedict XVI, calling himself a pilgrim, spoke of his faith to an assembled crowd of about 150,000; set in the context of the Year of Faith, his words are genuinely inspirational.

"I have felt like Saint Peter with the Apostles in the boat on the Sea of Galilee. The Lord has given us many days of sunshine and gentle breeze, days in which the catch has been abundant; there have been times when the seas were rough and the wind against us, as in the whole history of the Church it has ever been—and the Lord seemed to sleep."

"Nevertheless, I always knew that the Lord is in the barque [boat], that the barque of the Church is not mine, not ours, but His—and He shall not let her sink. It is He who steers her; to be sure, he does so also through men of His choosing, for he desired that it be so. This was and is a certainty that nothing can tarnish. It is for this reason that today my heart is filled with gratitude to God, for never did He leave me or the Church without His consolation, His Light, His love."

• 36 •

Assessing "Filipino Faith" Today

In January 2013, the Bishops of the Philippines (CBCP) issued a lengthy pastoral exhortation entitled: "Lord, Increase Our Faith!" This reflective document, issued for the Year of Faith, assesses the strengths and weaknesses of the faith as practiced by ordinary Filipinos.

The bishops assert: "We need to look into the kind of faith we have. Is our faith one that possesses the mind and heart? A faith that flows into daily life such that our private and public life demonstrates our being true disciples of the Lord?"

The bishops evaluate **both** the "positive and negative qualities" of faith. "In truth, our Filipino faith is deep and simple. We are not embarrassed to perform religious rites, like making the sign of the cross…."

However, the bishops state: "Our faith is separated from life; we do not practice our faith…. That is why in our predominantly Christian country, poverty, social injustice and lack of integrity are glaring." Clearly, the bishops are seeking to deepen the faith of Filipinos; their call to renewal is equally valid for all Christians.

Integral Faith Formation is Essential

The Philippine Bishops' (CBCP) 2013 pastoral exhortation for the Year of Faith seeks a genuine renewal in the faith of all Catholics. The bishops provide several clear emphases that form the basis of such a profound renewal.

"The weaknesses of our faith and the challenges facing it summon us to renewed integral evangelization, to new evangelization with new fervor, new methods, and new expressions. This is the rationale for integral faith formation."

This renewal is a long-term process that "seeks and leads to maturity in faith, a faith that is informed and lived, a faith committed to the mission of announcing the Gospel of Jesus, including participation in the work of justice and social transformation."

"We need conversion and renewal…. But, it is not enough to have an intellectual knowledge of the faith. What is absolutely imperative is a personal, loving knowledge of the Lord Jesus. He is the center of our faith!" Renewed faith must always be anchored in "a life of discipleship."

• 38 •

Forget Fear, Find Faith

What is the opposite of "faith" in sacred scripture? Is it doubt, disbelief, skepticism, or mistrust? One may validly assert that the antonym of "faith" is **"fear."** To be afraid means doubting God and his loving presence in our lives.

The admonition "Do not be afraid" appears frequently in the Bible. At the Annunciation, Gabriel says: "Mary, do not be afraid; you have won God's favor" (Lk 1:30). "Joseph, son of David, do not be afraid to take Mary home as your wife, because she has conceived what is in her by the Holy Spirit" (Mt 1:20).

At the birth of Christ, the lowly shepherds hear the angel declare: "Do not be afraid; I bring you news of great joy" (Lk 2:10). During the storm at sea, Jesus says: "Courage! It is I! Do not be afraid" (Mk 6:50).

All these biblical characters had to *move from fear to faith*, surrendering to God's loving plan for them. Our doubts and fears are real; we must face them. Yet, we receive the same invitation from Jesus to believe. Our motto of discipleship is the "4-F" approach: **Forget Fear, Find Faith!**

• 39 •

Appreciating Our Parents' Faith

The "sense of the faithful" (*sensus fidelium*), a term originating in the early Church, refers to the truth sensed or recognized by the entire body of the faithful under the guidance of the *magisterium*. It is part of a theology of the laity within a full understanding of the Church.

This teaching concretely means that we can look to our own parents and other practicing Catholics to perceive the essence of Christian faith. For example, a mother who volunteers one half-day each week to serve an invalid neighbor lady intuitively knows the meaning of faith. The same mother who prays thirty minutes each evening gives a powerful example to her family.

A father who stops all his farm work to assure that the family gets to Mass every Sunday deeply senses the meaning of faith. Indeed, many ordinary Catholics intuitively have this *sensus fidelium*. Who are such role models of faith for you? How have they influenced your faith journey? Thank God for them (as I thank God for my parents whose lives I have described here). *Deo gratias!*

PRESIDENT CORAZON AQUINO

• 40 •

Capturing "Faith" in Poetry

Several years ago I discovered this little "poem" simply entitled "Faith" by Karen Taylor; it captures some of the important dynamics of our journey in Christian faith. The poem contrasts a fear-filled response to life with one that is inspired by faith.

We struggle to keep up the pace.
Sometimes we wonder why.
Fear says we'll never win the race.
But faith tells us to try.

There's no one there to comfort us.
We're lost and all alone.
Fear drives us far away from God.
But faith brings us back home.

We need to place our trust in Him,
Although we cannot see.
Our fears can bind us evermore,
But faith will set us free.

To walk in faith or run in fear …
It's up to us to choose.
To walk in faith will win the race,
To run in fear will lose.

• 41 •

Abraham: Our Father in Faith

All three great monotheistic religions (Judaism, Christianity, and Islam) honor Abraham for his profound faith. The Church's First Eucharistic Prayer speaks of "Abraham, our father in faith."

Abraham's faith is manifested in his willingness to leave his own country and set out for a land that God would show him (cf. Gen 12). He is asked to believe that his elderly wife Sarah, unable to bear children, would give birth to a son (cf. Gen 18). He is tested by God when asked to be willing to sacrifice his beloved son (cf. Gen 22).

Abraham is a model of faith (cf. Heb 11:8-12) because he responded to God's invitation with radical obedience and trust. He, like us, often walked in darkness, having only the light of God's promise and fidelity, not having complete understanding or clarity.

Faith means loving and knowing the God who leads us. Succinctly stated, "faith means *not* knowing what the future holds, but knowing *who* holds the future." Abraham's faith was tested and proven true; as all genuine faith, it was anchored on the person of the one true God.

Prayer: Rooted in Living Faith

To address God as "Our Father" is already an act of faith; it reflects both our relationship to God and to others. Jesus taught his disciples this prayer on different occasions. The New Testament preserves two versions—one by Matthew (6:9-13) and one by Luke (11:2-4).

Because Jesus the Lord taught this prayer to his disciples, it is known as the "Lord's Prayer." Tertullian called it "the summary of the whole Gospel," and Saint Thomas Aquinas said it is "the most perfect of all prayers."

The first half of the Our Father expresses our faith by praising God, asking that "your kingdom come, your will be done." The second half is a faith-filled prayer of petition: "Give us this day...."

One might even draw a parallelism between the two parts of the Lord's prayer and the two basic commandments to love God and neighbor. Faith demands that we submit to God who is a loving Father and also manifest our faith in ready service to neighbor. Only in faith can we ask God: "Forgive us our sins as we forgive those who sin against us."

Faith Implores God's Generosity

Sincere prayer is an act of faith, believing in God's goodness to all humanity and creation. The second half of the "Lord's Prayer" consists of four petitions; we ask for the good things we all need.

When we Christians in faith express our needs to our Father, we are also committing ourselves to making our prayer requests a reality. Praying for our daily bread means doing our part in relieving hunger and deprivation in the world. We ask forgiveness with the sincere promise to forgive others.

We also ask that we would not be led into temptation and be delivered from evil. Here we are not asking that we never be tested or tried; in fact, God allows testing as a way of determining the depth and genuineness of our faith.

Our prayer is simply asking that we be spared from being tested beyond our capacity to endure trials and tribulations. As we plead for this grace, we also commit ourselves to "bear each other's burdens" (Gal 6:2) and remain in solidarity with others who are experiencing life's difficult challenges.

• 44 •

Trusting God in Hard Times

The Bible provides examples of people of great faith. The experience of Job is a story of endurance, patience, and true faith.

All Job's children were killed when a freak windstorm collapsed their house. His workers were brutally murdered and all his livestock were stolen or destroyed. His own health was taken from him. He was falsely accused and tormented by his "friends" who asserted that these tribulations were due to Job's hidden sinfulness.

Job's faith-response is classic. He says: "Naked I came forth from my mother's womb, and naked shall I go back again. The Lord gave and the Lord has taken away; blessed be the name of the Lord." Scripture adds: "In all this Job did not sin, nor did he say anything disrespectful of God" (Job 1:21-22).

Faced with his dire and tragic situation, Job would not blame or curse God (as his wife suggested he should). Thus, he is a unique example of faith and submission to God's "truly inscrutable designs." He never stopped loving and believing in God. Job, saint of hard times, strengthen our faith.

• 45 •

Faith in God's Unfathomable Call

The Old Testament prophet Jeremiah was a fiery person. When the Lord called him, he protested that he was too young and did not know how to speak. God reminded Jeremiah that even when he was still in his mother's womb, he was already known; God himself would give him words to speak.

Jeremiah's mission was very difficult; his task was "to root up and to tear down, to destroy and to demolish, to build and to plant" (Jer 1:10). He had to preach about the coming plagues and destruction of Jerusalem as punishment for Israel's multiple infidelities. This God-given task brought him threats, harassment, persecution, arrests, imprisonment, and even exile to Egypt.

Jeremiah's deep faith meant that he had to constantly live with many unanswered questions. Yet, this faith gave him the strength to trust that God was in control. As Christian believers, we too have God's assurance: "I will never forsake you or abandon you" (Heb 13:5). We know that "for those who love God all things work together for good" (Rom 8:28).

• 46 •

Joseph: Model of Persistent Faith

The "Joseph story" is narrated in *Genesis*, the first book of the Bible. Son of Jacob and Rachel, Joseph is sold by his own brothers into slavery and is taken to Egypt. Enduring many sufferings, he eventually is given a prominent position by Pharaoh.

A severe famine spreads across the area. Even Joseph's own family needs to turn to Egypt for help. They never realized that God, through their evil designs against Joseph, had sent him ahead to save them.

When Joseph reveals himself to his brothers, he says: "Do not be afraid…. Even though you intended to do harm to me, God intended it for good, to achieve his present end…. So, have no fear; I myself will provide for you…."

Yes, in faith, we believe that God often takes humanity's misfortune and sinfulness and changes them into opportunities for grace. God is truly God; he does not return evil for offense; he answers with love. Even when we face life's vicissitudes, can we, like Joseph, pray: Lord, I believe in your love; I know you will bring good out of this difficult situation!

• 47 •

An Asian Witness of Deep Faith

Vietnamese Cardinal Nguyen Van Thuan (1928-2002) was a prisoner, often in solitary confinement, for thirteen years. His own words capture the depth of his faith.

When arrested he immediately recalled the experience of Maryknoll Bishop James E. Walsh, imprisoned for twelve years in China. For Cardinal Nguyen Van Thuan, his imprisonment would be "a turning point in my life…. I will live the present moment and fill it with love."

"When the Communists put me in the hold of the boat, the *Hai-Phong*, along with 1,500 other prisoners and moved us to the North, I said to myself: 'Here is my cathedral, here are the people God has given me to care for, here is my mission: to ensure the presence of God among these, my despairing, miserable brothers. It is God's will that I am here. I accept his will'."

In prison he obtained some wine disguised as medicine; he writes: "I will never be able to express the joy that was mine: each day, with three drops of wine, a drop of water in the palm of my hand, I celebrated my Mass." Profound and Genuine Faith!

• 48 •

An African Woman of Faith and Forgiveness

Saint Josephine Bakhita (1869-1947) was kidnapped at age nine by slave-traders, beaten until she bled, and sold five times in the slave-markets of Sudan. Finally, she was bought by an Italian merchant and brought to Italy, where she received religious instruction, was baptized, and joined the Canossian Sisters. Written in later life, her first-person narrative is a remarkable testimony of faith.

Bakhita described her excruciating ordeal of tattooing: "My face was spared, but six patterns were designed on my breasts and sixty more on my belly and arms. I thought I would die, especially when salt was poured in the wounds…. It was by a miracle of God I didn't die. He had destined me for better things."

"I enjoyed the opportunity [in Italy] to be instructed in the Christian faith…. The saintly sisters helped me know God, whom I had experienced in my heart since childhood…. Now at last I knew Him…. I am definitely loved and whatever happens to me—I am awaited by this Love. And so my life is good." A remarkable faith-journey: from slavery to sanctity!

• 49 •

Damien: Herald of Joyful Faith

The missionary dedication and heroic service to the lepers in Hawaii by Damien de Veuster are well known. In his life one finds verified a simple verse of scripture: "The love of Christ urges us" (2 Cor 5:14).

What is particularly striking is the profound joy Damien experienced in providing hope for the people he served. In a November 9, 1887 letter he wrote to his brother: "The joy and contentment of heart that the Sacred Hearts deluge me with, make me consider myself the happiest missioner in the world."

Indeed, deep joy and profound faith mark Saint Damien's life. Writing to his family from Molokai (November 25, 1873), he noted: "I find my greatest happiness in serving the Lord in his poor and sick children—who are rejected by others" [words inscribed on Damien's tomb in the Louvain church crypt].

Damien, the joyful evangelizer who lived his faith with his leper community in Molokai, calls himself the "happiest missioner in the world"; he remains a contemporary witness of profound—and joyful—faith.

• 50 •

Cory Aquino: Courageous Faith

Maria Corazon Sumulong Cojuangco served as the seventh president of the Republic of the Philippines (1986-1992); she was the first woman to hold that office as well as the first female president in Asia. August 1, 2009 marked her passing.

In the volumes of *Speeches of President Corazon C. Aquino*, one is often struck by Cory's faith and courage. She noted the aptness of the phrase "People's Power," but said that a better term might be "Prayer Power" (June 6, 1986). "And it is by faith that we proceed on the longer journey we have yet to take to bring progress, prosperity and justice to our land" (March 12, 1987).

Cory spoke of the values that guided her life and should distinguish the Filipino nation: "faith in God and in the power of prayer, industry and honesty, love of country, and respect for the unity of the family" (June 18, 1988).

Without ambiguity, Cory anchored her life and mission in the faith, prayer, courage and hope that shaped her life. In a word, Cory proved to be a genuine leader, a spiritual beacon of faith.

• 51 •

Maximilian Kolbe: Sacrificial Faith

With deep faith, Maximilian endured the extreme horrors of Auschwitz, the notorious Nazi concentration camp in Poland. His final act of Christian witness came on July 30, 1941.

When Franciszek Gajowniczek was randomly chosen to die by starvation, he cried out: "My poor wife and children! I will never see them again." Father Kolbe volunteered to take his place. Asked by the commandant who he was, Kolbe replied: "I am a Catholic priest." Kolbe's offer was accepted.

Franciszek survived and lived to be 95 years old. When Pope John Paul II canonized Kolbe on October 10, 1982 in Saint Peter's Square, Franciszek, along with other Auschwitz survivors, was present (as was this writer).

Today, when one visits the Auschwitz concentration camp, one sees the paschal candle prominently displayed in the middle of the underground starvation cell. What a moving sight! The candle, symbol of Christ's own death and resurrection, touches the core of Christian faith—your faith, my faith, the faith of Father Kolbe.

SAINT MAXIMILIAN KOLBE

Marian Faith: Immaculate Conception

Pope Pius IX in *Ineffabilis Deus* on December 8, 1854 wrote: "We declare, pronounce and define: the doctrine which holds that the most Blessed Virgin Mary was, from the first moment of her conception, by a singular grace and privilege of almighty God and in view of the merits of Christ Jesus the Savior of the human race, preserved immune from all stain of original sin."

Pope Paul VI described Mary's Immaculate Conception by noting: "It was the Holy Spirit who filled Mary with grace in the very first moment of her conception…, making her the Immaculate One."

The Immaculate Conception does not signify a special grace that was given to Mary at some later point of her life; it describes her person, her nature—from the beginning of her existence. She can truly say (as she did to Bernadette at Lourdes): I *am* the Immaculate Conception. Mary's whole being becomes a temple of God; the Holy Spirit dwells in her in a very special way. The Church's Marian dogmas are among the most beautiful elements of our faith!

• 53 •

Ordinary Christians and Marian Faith

Catholics readily assent to the Church's teaching regarding Marian dogmas, although they probably are unable to explain the nuances of the individual doctrines.

In addition, Catholics have a deep faith in Mary's intercessory role, commonly manifested in novena prayers, especially to Our Lady of Perpetual Help. I treasure an experience I had as a boy which manifested the deep Marian faith of my father, an ordinary farmer.

Henry Lippert, my father's very close friend, fell in love and married a Lutheran lady. Henry stopped going to the Catholic Church. Many years later Henry suddenly died of a heart attack while working in the fields on his farm. My father was called to retrieve Henry's body; then, it was discovered that he had a well-worn rosary in the pocket of his pants.

My father told me: "We don't have to worry about Henry; he will reach heaven. He was faithful to Mary, so she will assure his entrance into heaven." Such is the deep—and admirable—Marian faith of many ordinary Catholics!

• 54 •

Mary: Star of Evangelization

The Second Vatican Council defined the Church as an "essentially missionary" community (AG 2). Then in 1975 Pope Paul VI updated the Church's mission theology in his beautiful apostolic exhortation *Evangelii Nuntiandi* (EN). In EN 82 Paul VI graces Mary with a "new" title: "Star of Evangelization." Popes John Paul II and Benedict XVI frequently note that Mary is "the Star of the New Evangelization."

Mary is the Star of Evangelization because she brought forth Jesus to the entire world. She carried the Word of God in her womb, not only on her lips; she radiated Christ by her very presence. Her one missionary desire was to lead people to Jesus.

Mary, enkindle in us a renewed enthusiasm for our faith. Inspire in us the courage and zeal to live the Gospel. Open our hearts to the Holy Spirit, enabling us to transform the world in the image of your Son. Walk with us in faith, strengthen us in hope, unite us in love. Enable us to become dynamic disciples-in-mission. You are our "Star of Evangelization"!

MARY, EXALTED IN GLORY

• 55 •

Certain Sign of Our Future Glory

The Assumption of Mary is the most recent formally defined dogma of the Church (1950). Pius XII declared: "Mary ever Virgin, when the course of her earthly life was finished, was taken up body and soul into the glory of heaven." The Church's faith affirms that Mary in the fullness of her historical personality now lives in union with the risen Christ.

This beautiful article of faith has universal significance: Mary fully participates in the new and everlasting life promised for the human race through the saving death and resurrection of Christ. Indeed, this very same hope of glory is promised to people of faith: "All will be brought to life in Christ" (1 Cor 15:22).

Catholic creeds affirm the resurrection of the body, Christ's body, our bodies. Mary's Assumption is further evidence that through God's grace, we, too, will share in Christ's ultimate victory over death. We experience profound peace, knowing we are assured of this great gift of eternal life— even as we journey midst the sufferings of our present life.

Pope Francis Speaks on Faith

The Acts of the Apostles (4:13-21) records an event when the apostles Peter and John had to face accusations from the Jewish Sanhedrin because they were boldly proclaiming the resurrection of Jesus. Pope Francis uses this passage to reflect on the fact that faith is "a grace, a gift of the Lord"; it is "a reality we have seen and heard."

Peter and John "stood firm in the faith," saying, "we cannot but speak of what we have seen and heard." Pope Francis continues: the apostles' testimony "reminds me of our faith. And, what is our faith like? Is it strong? Or is it at times a little like rosewater, a somewhat watered-down faith? When problems arise, are we brave like Peter or inclined to be lukewarm?" Peter's example, the pope asserts, teaches us that "faith is not negotiable."

Pope Francis suggests a daily prayer for us: "Lord, thank you so much for my faith. Preserve my faith, increase it. May my faith be strong and courageous. And, help me in moments when, like Peter and John, I must make it public."

POPE FRANCIS

• 57 •

Pope John XXIII's Bold Faith

When John XXIII announced in 1959 his ambitious plan to convoke Vatican II, he was already 77 years old. To seek a "new Pentecost" and a profound renewal (*aggiornamento*) of the Church demanded courageous faith.

"Good Pope John," as he was popularly known, further expressed his faith convictions in his opening Council speech in 1962. He said the idea of a Council unexpectedly came to him as "a flash of heavenly light" that would unleash "spiritual riches" and "new energies" in the Church.

The pope optimistically believed that "Divine Providence" was guiding the entire endeavor. Thus, he noted that he felt he "must disagree with those prophets of gloom, who are always forecasting disaster, as though the end of the world were at hand."

Seeking renewed Gospel proclamation, John noted: "The substance of the ancient doctrine of the deposit of faith is one thing, and the way in which it is presented is another." With profound faith John XXIII saw the Council as a "rising day" that "breathes sanctity and arouses great joy"!

• 58 •

Continuing the Year of Faith

The Church's Year of Faith has concluded, yet we can always renew our commitment to continue our "faith-journey." The pastoral letter of Cardinal Luis A. Tagle on the Year of Faith offers genuinely helpful insights for us as "pilgrims in faith."

The Cardinal writes: "In our time, the Second Vatican Council is the great moment of renewal in faith. Blessed John XXIII desired that through the Council 'the Church will become greater in spiritual riches..., she will look to the future without fear'."

"In a span of fifty years after Vatican II, the world has seen dramatic changes.... But we also believe that the contemporary world ... expresses its search for God in ways that the Church must also discover."

Thus, as an enduring fruit of the Year of Faith, we are challenged to "listen to the deep cries and aspirations of the people and societies of our time so that we can proclaim Jesus Christ to them with new methods, new expressions and new fervor." True faith demands continual "listening and mission." Undoubtedly, *every year must be a year of faith!*

Faith Proclaims: Christ is Our King

The theme of Christ's Lordship is integral to the New Testament message and Christian faith. When Pilate questions Jesus about his authority, Jesus asserts his true Lordship, noting, "Mine is not a kingdom of this world" (Jn 18:36).

Pope Francis' encyclical *Lumen Fidei* [18] provides many insights on how Christians affirm their faith in Christ, Lord and King. "In faith, Christ is not simply the one in whom we believe, the supreme manifestation of God's love; he is also the one with whom we are united precisely in order to believe."

Accepting Jesus as Lord means both "believing" Jesus and "believing in" Jesus. As Pope Francis writes: "We 'believe' Jesus when we accept his word, his testimony, because he is truthful. We 'believe in' Jesus when we personally welcome him into our lives and journey towards him, clinging to him in love and following in his footsteps along the way."

Accepting in faith that Jesus is King "leads us, as Christians, to live our lives in this world with ever greater commitment and intensity."

• 60 •

Faith without Mission is Dead

Saint James in his letter forcefully notes that without good works faith is "quite dead" (Jas 2:17). In a similar fashion Pope Francis in his message for World Mission Day 2013, demonstrates that genuine faith is necessarily a missionary faith.

"Faith is God's precious gift ... that one cannot keep to oneself.... If we want to keep it only to ourselves, we will become isolated, sterile and sick Christians.... Missionary outreach is a clear sign of the maturity of an ecclesial community."

"The Second Vatican Council emphasized in a special way how the missionary task, that of broadening the boundaries of faith, belongs to every baptized person and all Christian communities." Mission is *not* "a secondary aspect of Christian life, but its essential aspect."

For Pope Francis, an active missionary commitment "is not merely a programmatic dimension in Christian life, but it is also a paradigmatic dimension that affects all aspects of Christian life." Pope Francis' powerful words challenge the depth of our "missionary faith."

Points to Ponder from *Lumen Fidei*
Pope Francis' Encyclical on Faith

"The Year of Faith was inaugurated on the fiftieth anniversary of the opening of the Second Vatican Council. This is itself a clear indication that Vatican II was a Council on faith.... The Second Vatican Council enabled the light of faith to illumine our human experience from within, accompanying the men and women of our time on their journey. It clearly showed how faith enriches life in all its dimensions" (6).

"There is an urgent need, then, to see once again that faith is a light, for once the flame of faith dies out, all other lights begin to dim. The light of faith is unique, since it is capable of illuminating every aspect of human existence.... Faith, received from God as a supernatural gift, becomes a light for our way, guiding our journey through time" (4).

"Believing means entrusting oneself to a merciful love which always accepts and pardons, which sustains and directs our lives, and which shows its power by its ability to make straight the crooked lines of our history" (13).

"Faith's way of seeing things is centered on Christ.... Faith does not merely gaze at Jesus, but sees things as Jesus himself sees them, with his own eyes: it is a participation in his way of seeing" (20, 18).

"Faith becomes operative in the Christian on the basis of the gift received, the love which attracts our hearts to Christ (cf. Gal 5:6), and enables us to become part of the Church's great pilgrimage through history until the end of the world" (22).

"Faith transforms the whole person precisely to the extent that he or she becomes open to love.... Faith's understanding is born when we receive the immense love of God which transforms us inwardly and enables us to see reality with new eyes" (26).

"The light of faith in Jesus also illumines the path of all those who seek God.... Anyone who sets off on the path of doing good to others is already drawing near to God, is already sustained by his help, for it is characteristic of the divine light to brighten the eyes whenever we walk towards the fullness of love" (35).

"The Church is a Mother who teaches us to speak the language of faith.... The love which is the Holy Spirit and which dwells in the Church unites every age and makes us contemporaries of Jesus, thus guiding us along our pilgrimage of faith" (38).

"The Eucharist is precious nourishment for faith: an encounter with Christ truly present in the supreme act of his love, the life-giving gift of himself.... In the Eucharist we learn to see the heights and depths of reality" (44).

"Faith is no refuge for the fainthearted, but something which enhances our lives. It makes us aware of a magnificent calling, the vocation of love. It assures us that this love is trustworthy and worth embracing, for it is based on God's faithfulness which is stronger than our every weakness" (53).

"When faith is weakened, the foundations of life also risk being weakened…. If we remove faith in God from our cities, mutual trust would be weakened; we would remain united only by fear and our stability would be threatened" (55).

"Christians know that suffering cannot be eliminated, yet it can have meaning and become an act of love and entrustment into the hands of God who does not abandon us; in this way it can serve as a moment of growth in faith and love" (56).

"Nor does the light of faith make us forget the sufferings of this world. How many men and women of faith have found mediators of light in those who suffer! So it was with Saint Francis of Assisi and the leper or with Blessed Mother Teresa of Calcutta and her poor" (57).

"Faith is not a light which scatters all our darkness, but a lamp which guides our steps in the night and suffices for the journey. To those who suffer, God does not provide arguments which explain everything; rather, his response is that of an accompanying presence …" (57).

RECENT BOOKS
BY JAMES H. KROEGER

THE GIFT OF MISSION.
Maryknoll, New York: Orbis Books, 2013.

A VATICAN II JOURNEY: FIFTY MILESTONES.
Makati City, Philippines: ST PAULS, 2012.

EXPLORING THE TREASURES OF VATICAN II.
Quezon City, Philippines: Claretian Publications and
Jesuit Communications, 2011.

THE DOCUMENTS OF VATICAN COUNCIL II.
Pasay City, Philippines: Paulines, 2011.

A FIERY FLAME: ENCOUNTERING GOD'S WORD.
Quezon City, Philippines: Claretian Publications,
Insta Publications, and Jesuit Communications, 2010.

THEOLOGY FROM THE HEART OF ASIA: I - II.
Quezon City, Philippines: Claretian Publications, 2008.

ONCE UPON A TIME IN ASIA:
STORIES OF HARMONY AND PEACE.
Maryknoll, New York: Orbis Books, 2006 [ten translations].

BECOMING LOCAL CHURCH: HISTORICAL,
THEOLOGICAL AND MISSIOLOGICAL ESSAYS.
Quezon City, Philippines: Claretian Publications, 2003.

THE FUTURE OF THE ASIAN CHURCHES:
THE ASIAN SYNOD AND *ECCLESIA IN ASIA*.
Quezon City, Philippines: Claretian Publications, 2002.

TELLING GOD'S STORY:
NATIONAL MISSION CONGRESS 2000.
Quezon City, Philippines: Claretian Publications, 2001.

TELL THE WORLD: CATECHETICAL MODULES
FOR MISSION ANIMATION.
Quezon City, Philippines: Claretian Publications, 2000.

ASIA-CHURCH IN MISSION.
Quezon City, Philippines: Claretian Publications, 1999.

LIVING MISSION: CHALLENGES IN
EVANGELIZATION TODAY.
Maryknoll, New York: Orbis Books, 1994, 2009.